CHESS *for* KIDS

Written and illustrated by Kelvin F. R. Smith
Chess consultant: Daniel C. Macdonald

ADAMS MEDIA CORPORATION
Holbrook, Massachusetts

Published by
Adams Media Corporation
260 Center Street, Holbrook, MA 02343

ISBN: 1-55850-792-2

Printed in China

J I H G F E D C B A

Produced by Somerville House Books Limited
3080 Yonge Street, Suite 5000, Ontario, Canada M4N 3N1

This book is available at quantity discounts for bulk purchases.
For information, call 1-800-872-5627 (in Massachusetts, 617-767-8100).

Visit our home page at http://www.adamsmedia.com

CONTENTS

Introduction	4	The Queen	30	Chess Terms	62
The Basic Rules	8	The King	34	Quiz Answers	64
The Kingdom	9	The Game	39		
The Pawn	10	Beginning the Game	40		
The Knight	16	The Middlegame	45		
The Bishop	20	The Endgame	50		
The Rook	24	How Games End	52		
Castling	28	Chess Notation	60		

INTRODUCTION

The King's Secret

There is a secret shared by every king that no one except his queen knows: the night before a battle, the king always has bad dreams. He awakes with a start. A cold sweat soaks his nightshirt, and his trembling hands clutch weakly at his neck. His eyes bulge with horror at the headsman's ax, which seems to float before his face. His ears ring with the awful voice of some rampaging rook or terrible queen who has just cried, "Checkmate!" and left him no way out. His queen patiently sighs and goes back to sleep. It's like this before every game, even though she's told him over and over that it has been centuries since any king *really* lost his head at the end of a battle.

"The king is dead" — that is what "checkmate" means. For well over a thousand years, chess kings have had to put up with excited enemies ruining many otherwise fine days with this unnerving announcement.

You see, chess is a battle played out between two armies, and the sole object of the game is to capture the enemy king. If that unfortunate king is captured, a resounding "checkmate" echoes across the battlefield. All the din of clashing pawn shields, of rambunctious rooks crashing their castles about, of rollicking knights leaping prankishly, of sly bishops wringing their hands in delight, and of queens shaking the ground with their mad rampages — all ends in that moment: the battle is over, and the kingdom is either won or lost.

The Game of Kings

When you play chess, you are like the general of the kingdom's army, guiding the various forces around the battlefield. It is a singularly unusual army, brimming with eccentric characters. But it is also a powerful legion, particularly when the pieces work in unison. We will meet them shortly: the stalwart pawns, the tempestuous rooks and the trickster knights, the cunning bishops and the fearsome queen, and finally, of course, the ever-fretting and ordinarily majestic king. But first we must consider the battlefield, the chessboard, and look at the basic rules of chess.

Only by playing chess again and again will you truly experience the game's magic, its secret forces, and its endless possibilities. Chess is not dependent on the whims of chance. Instead it requires strategy, scheming, tactics, and a mix of clever planning, foresight, caution, and courage. It is a game full of surprises, and it survives as the most wonderful and exciting game in the world, two thousand years after it first replaced real battlefields.

Opposing Forces

Because there are two armies in chess, you always need two players. One is called "white" and can move only the light pieces. The other player is called "black" and can move only the dark pieces.

The Chessboard

To the beginner, the chessboard looks like an ordinary checkerboard, eight squares wide and eight squares deep, alternating light and dark. It is, in fact, a mysterious surface. In time, as you learn to play, you will be able to tell which of the sixty-four squares is weak and which are really powerful. The board is placed so that both players have a white square in the bottom right-hand corner. Each player has eight pawns and eight royal pieces at their command. They are shown here with the symbols that represent them in chess diagrams. These symbols are used all over the world so that everyone can recognize them.

one king

one queen

two rooks

two bishops

two knights

eight pawns

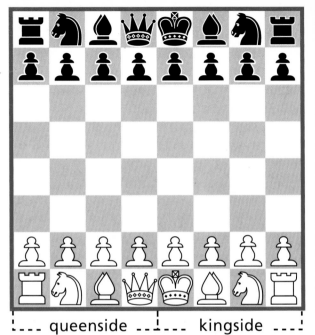

queenside   kingside

In their opening position, both queens and kings face each other across the chessboard. We therefore speak of a queenside and a kingside to the board.

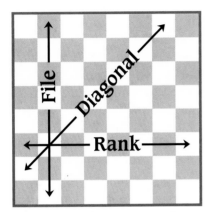

We call a row of squares across the board a rank; a row of squares up the board a file; and a line of same colored squares joined at the corners a diagonal. These terms are important for describing how pieces move and capture.

Getting Started

To decide who plays black and who plays white, one player takes two pawns, one of each color, and hides one in each hand. The other player chooses a hand and becomes the color of the pawn chosen. With each successive game, players swap sides.

Once you have chosen your color, set up the board as illustrated. Make sure that the rook in the lower right-hand corner is sitting on a white square. Also check that the bishops and the knights are on either side of the king and queen. Finally, check that the queen is on the center square of her own color. In this way, the two queens will stare at each other across the board, as will the two kings.

The chessboard is now set up and ready for play!

Attack and Defense

The object of the game is to checkmate the other player's king. This happens when the king cannot escape capture on the next turn.

Naturally, each side tries to defend its king as nobly as possible, while also trying to weaken the opponent's forces. They do this by capturing enemy pieces. A successful capture undermines an army's ability to protect its king and weakens its strength to attack. Astute chess players will make sure that one of their pieces cannot be captured unless they can capture an opponent piece of equal or more importance. In this way, a game develops with many exchanges.

7

The Basic Rules

Each piece moves and captures in its own special way. *All* pieces, though, observe the basic rules of chess.

Making a Move

When a player touches a piece on his or her turn, that piece must be moved, if it can be moved legally. (Beginners sometimes waive this rule. If you do, just be sure to agree on it first.)

A move cannot be taken back. It is always completed when the piece has been moved and the player takes his or her hand off that piece.

There are nine basic rules:

1. White always moves first.
2. Players then take turns. When it is your turn, you must move one piece of your own color. You cannot skip a turn.
3. You can move only one piece in a turn, and it moves only once, except when castling (see page 28).
4. Except for the knight, no piece can jump over another piece, except in the special case of castling when the Rook jumps over the King.
5. A capture is made when you move a piece onto a square occupied by an opponent's piece. That piece is then immediately removed from the board. Only one piece can be taken in a single turn.
6. You are not obligated to take an opponent's piece just because that piece is exposed to being taken.
7. You are not allowed to make a move that exposes your own king to being captured on the following turn. (If a move is made in this way, it is said to be illegal and it must be taken over again properly.)
8. If your opponent's king is directly exposed to capture, you can say, "Check." Your opponent must then remove the king from check on the next move. This can be done by moving the king, putting a piece in the way, or capturing the checking piece.
9. The object of the game is to "checkmate" the other player's king. A king is checkmate when he cannot escape capture on the next turn. A game can also end in a "stalemate" or a "draw."

The Kingdom

THE PAWN

Pawns always look serious. It's a most important job they have, and it's a dangerous world out there since everyone else is so much taller. Can you imagine the pawns before the bugle summons them to the chess field? They are the ordinary people of the kingdom: the butchers, the bakers, the dragon-keepers, the lawyers, even the candlestick makers. But once on the chessboard, they all look identical, and their eyes glare fiercely ahead from beneath their brows in anticipation of the grave tasks that lie ahead.

At the beginning of the contest, all eight pawns stand side by side, spanning the width of the battlefield, blinking in unison and staring at eight enemy pawns. They never turn their heads. They can only march forward in a straight line, unless they are capturing a piece. They advance just one square at a time, except for the first time they move. On its first move each pawn may show a special burst of energy and advance two squares.

To capture a piece, a pawn moves one space forward diagonally, to the left or right. After it displaces the opponent piece in the neighboring file, it continues to advance forward on that file — unless, of course, it strikes again.

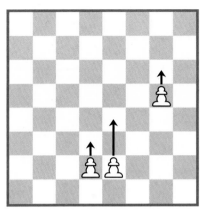

*All pawns can move either one or two squares forward from their starting squares.

* After a pawn's first move, it can move forward only one square each turn.

* Pawns capture opposing pieces by moving one square diagonally forward left or right.

* Pawns can never move backward or sideways and never forward if blocked.

The center pawns, those in front of the king and queen, are often the first in the game to move. It's their task to control those critical four squares in the center of the board. They share this job with the sliding bishops and leaping knights, but pawns are not in the habit of requesting assistance from their royal warriors. Instead they set about defending each other by standing on diagonally adjacent squares. By organizing themselves this way, they build a very important defensive structure known as a pawn chain. Because these chains are difficult for the enemy to disrupt or to cross, they can guard entire sections of the board from intrusion. Pawn chains are especially desirable in front of a king, who might be watching the game unfold from a corner of the board.

Naturally, it's very pleasing to a pawn's delicate sensibilities when it becomes the center of attention. And when a pawn captures a very tall opponent, everybody is surprised.

The pawn will say it was just doing its duty, while reminding everyone repeatedly and again about the conquest. But nothing compares to the noise a pawn makes as it is about to reach the other end of the board.

As soon as a pawn crosses the center line of the board, it presents a new danger to the other side. The eyes of an enemy rook might glint as they are turned upon this pesky intruder, especially if this pawn is a passed pawn, that is, a pawn that can keep advancing on its file with no opposing pawn to stop it. You see, if the pawn reaches the other end of the board, it will not fall off the edge or anything like that. Instead, when it steps on the last square, a pawn is immediately promoted to any piece it wants to be, except a king. Such pawn promotions often lead to decisive victories.

Pawn Strategy Tips

* At the beginning of the game, use your king and queen pawns to gain control of the four center squares.

* Try not to advance more than three pawns in the opening of the game. Your remaining pawns might have to protect the king.

* Avoid advancing your pawns too far beyond the center line in the early stages of the game. They can become isolated and hard to defend.

* Where possible, avoid doubling your pawns on a single file. Pawns are strongest on adjacent files.

* Build diagonal pawn chains. They give you more control of the board and are harder for your opponent to break through.

* Protect all your pawns. They are important.

The pawn captures enemy pawns and pieces by moving forward diagonally, left or right.

The Humble Pawn

The word pawn comes from the Old French word *peon*. It refers to the common folk, the ordinary people, the bakers and the smiths and the farmers, who became foot soldiers in times of battle.

"Pawn Chains"

Pawns learn to protect each other by forming pawn chains. A queen would think twice about bothering any opponent pawn in this diagram. Only the white pawn on the a file is entirely without support.

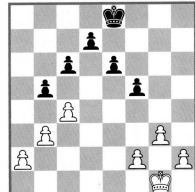

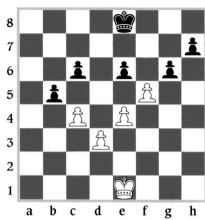

QUIZ — What black pawn can a white pawn take without itself being captured on the next move? (For quiz answers, see page 64.)

You're Promoted!
Any pawn that reaches the 8th rank is immediately promoted to any piece of the same color except a king.

En Passant

Now we come to one of the most peculiar rules in chess. There are not many such rules, and you won't need to worry about this one too often. The rule is called *en passant*. When a pawn moves two squares on its first move and lands next to an enemy pawn, that enemy pawn can capture and remove the pawn by moving to the square the pawn just moved through. The enemy pawn can only do this on the very next move. Capturing *en passant* is optional (unless it is the only legal move).

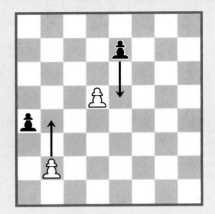

Fixed Pawns?

Opposing pawns who meet head on (on the same file) are famous for their legendary staring matches. Neither pawn can move unless one captures another piece, or is captured by another piece. Such pawns are known as fixed pawns.

THE KNIGHT

Beware of the knight, especially if he appears to be thinking. The knight is the merry prankster of the chessboard, the mischief maker, ever planning new tricks and surprises to spring on the enemy king. Perhaps you expected him to be a brave, lance-wielding warrior, his armor shining brilliantly in the sun, high atop a powerful stallion. Well, he is a little bit of this. But what kind of person rides a horse that can't even jump in a straight line?

And jump the horse does, leaping and bounding high over other warriors, sometimes even hopping over the head of an indignant king. Only on the square where he lands will a witless enemy feel the crush of the knight's mighty bulk, and be sent limping off the field. But the knight's jump is crooked — L-shaped, in fact — two squares forward or backward and one to the left or right. Technically put, the knight always lands on a square of the opposite color and on a different rank and file from the square he leaps from.

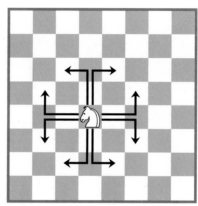

* The knight can jump over any piece and cannot be blocked.
* Knights can threaten up to eight squares at a time.
* Knights do not capture any piece or pieces they jump over.

At the beginning of a match, the knight stands between the bishop and rook, twitching in anticipation, since he is often the first of his neighbors to burst on the field. Aided by advancing pawns and bishops, he eagerly battles for control of the center of the board.

When the enemy begins to organize a defense, the knight's eyes twinkle in delight, and his smile grows ever wider. His path cannot be blocked. With a single bounce, he kicks dust behind opposing pawns, taunting the enemy king and rooks, happily spreading confusion throughout their ranks. His unique ability to jump makes him very hard to catch — unless he meets another knight.

The impish knight is always planning his favorite trick — the fork. Other warriors may play this trick, too, but the knight plays it best. Because he can bound onto squares that cannot be reached by anyone else, his arrival is almost always a shock. And since his path cannot be blocked, he can threaten up to eight squares at a time. As a result he can challenge two or more pieces. Should one of these be the queen and the other be the king, you can be sure his horse neighs with delight as the knight bellows, "Check." The king, being in check, wrings his hands in self-pity and scurries off to safety, leaving his horrified queen to the thoughtful knight . . .

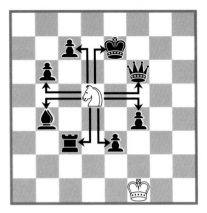

The knight can threaten up to eight pieces at the same time.

A Symbol of Chess

Because it is so easily recognized, the knight's horse has become one of the most popular symbols for chess. It has even been used with the Olympic logo, since, around the world, every two years, chess matches are held as an organized Olympic sport.

Knight Strategy Tips

* Use both knights early in the game to control the four center squares of the board and to defend any pawns you may have there.
* Avoid moving your knights to the edge of the board in your opening moves, since this will reduce their effectiveness and possibly trap them.
* Because the knight can jump, he is particularly good at defending and attacking pieces on a crowded board.
* The knight excels at attacking two opposing pieces at the same time in a "fork."

This knight was lost nine hundred years ago, when a Viking ship sank near Scotland. It was part of a chess set found in 1860 by a farmer. Upon discovering it, he ran away, thinking he had disturbed a fairy mound. The pieces were rescued by his more sensible wife and are now treasured in the British Museum.

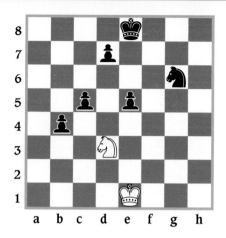

QUIZ — What pawn can the white knight take and not be taken itself in the next move?

Which Will It be?

Because the knight is checking the king and attacking the queen, the king must move, leaving the knight free to take the queen. This is known as a "royal fork."

THE BISHOP

Ordinary bishops are usually quite harmless. But chess bishops are by no means ordinary.
They are just a little bit nasty. They have cold shifty eyes and rarely smile. And when they do, it's a toothy grin that makes your hair stand on end. As the game begins, both bishops seem to be quietly daydreaming on either side of their king and queen. They are, in fact, conjuring up the most gruesome visions of the battle to follow.

To understand bishops, consider the way they see things. They never look forward or backward, or from side to side. They see things only from an angle, and they refuse to move on anything but a diagonal. Bishops of the same kingdom never even look at one another! Both advise and watch over the king, but never at the same time, and they never ever watch over each other. You'd almost think they didn't like one another.

You see, according to the rules, a bishop must move only along diagonal lines. As a result, each

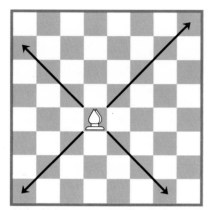

* The bishop moves on diagonals across as many empty squares as he wishes.
* Each player has one bishop on a black square and one on a white square.
* A bishop always remains on squares of the same color he starts on.

bishop must remain on squares of the same color as the one it started on. One bishop is always on black squares, while the other is always on white squares. This is the reason they can never protect each other.

Always aware of the king's need to castle (see pages 28-29), a bishop is eager to move into action and clear the way for the king and the rook. First, of course, one of his two diagonal paths of movement must be open and not blocked by his own pawns. It is a bad bishop indeed who lets such pawns remain inattentive, without giving them a good knock on their helmets with his handy crook.

As grumpy as bishops seem to be, bishops and pawns are really good friends. Indeed, they often team up with a knight at the start of a game and battle for control of the four center squares of the board. And as the pieces move around the board, one of the bishop's favorite pastimes is to lurk in a distant shadowy corner, quietly booing the opposing forces, until the opportunity arises to capture an unaware opponent by streaking gleefully across the field. Because they move on a diagonal, over as many empty squares as they wish, they are very good at capturing unwary rooks still sitting idly on their corner squares.

In spite of their quirks, bishops do sometimes work together. Sort of. If two bishops stand side by side, or one in front of the other, in the center of the field, they do a very good job at covering a large area, threatening four diagonals each. Near the end of a game, a pair of bishops can bully an enemy king into a corner, setting him up for a quick crushing checkmate from a flying knight! That's when they beam with their toothy smiles and contemplate what extraordinary bishops they really are!

Bishop Strategy Tips

* Move your bishops early in the game. By doing so, you will gain more control of the four center squares and open your back rank for castling.
* Do not block your bishops behind pawns on the same colored squares as your bishop.
* Position your bishops near your corner diagonal squares.
* Using your bishops together gives you better control of the board.
* Use bishops to defend your passed pawns, because each pawn can become a queen.

The bishop can threaten up to four pieces at once.

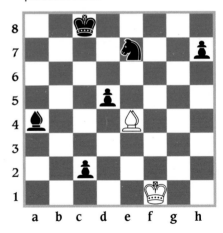

The Bishop Is a Fool!

In the long history of chess, there was once a piece that represented a pair of elephant's tusks. When the game was introduced to Europe, the English thought this piece looked like a bishop's hat, while the French thought it looked like a jester's cap. In French the bishop is known as *le fou*, or the fool.

QUIZ — What pawn can the white bishop take and still not be taken itself in the next move?

A Bad Bishop

A bishop whose effectiveness is reduced by its own pawns is a bad bishop. In the above diagram, white's bishop is not only blocked in by its own pawns, but is also preventing white's king from castling into a strong defensive position. Not only that, but the king wants a cup of tea with the rook!

THE ROOK

When a rook gets upset, he goes berserk. In the early stages of the game, it's easy to think of the rook as a quiet, easygoing, almost lazy fellow, the kind who sits at home while everyone else is out on the playing field. From his tower at a corner of the board, behind a row of defending pawns, he watches the game develop: cheering for the knights as they urge their mighty horses onto the field, waving to the bishops as they angle across the board. As the queen moves forward, he salutes her and vows to protect her king while she's away from his side.

Once the queen and other pieces have moved into positions farther up the board, the king is left exposed. With no one at his side, he may become a bit nervous and decide that the time has come to castle. Castling is a special defensive move that can only be made once. It's the only time in which two pieces (the king and one of the rooks) move on the same turn.

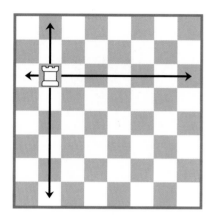

* Rooks move on ranks left or right over any number of empty squares.
* Rooks can also move forward or backward on a file over any number of empty squares.
* The rook is used in castling.

When the king decides to castle, he makes sure the conditions for castling are just right. (These conditions are described on page 28.) He then chooses one of his rooks and moves two squares toward him. The chosen rook then instantly scoots around to the first square on the other side of the king, ready to protect him against anyone who approaches from that side. This position is very comfortable for both the king and the rook, since they usually have a wall of three trusty pawns in front of them. Because they are quite safe here, the rook can relax and keep the king and the pawns company, making tea for them, chatting, and only occasionally going up his tower, where he can look out over the field, keeping an eye on the game's progress.

But don't be fooled by this. When the board starts to open up, it's time for the rook to get involved. Then this rather quiet, easygoing castle guard undergoes a change in character.

If one of his friends is in danger, the rook gets, well, just a little bit wild. His eyes swell to the size of teacups, and he charges into action. Nose twitching, chest heaving, and eyes blazing, the rook heaves his tower up over his head and thunders up and down whole files and across entire ranks, picking off passed pawns, forcing knights and bishops to scurry to safety, and crashing into opposing rooks with a force that makes the whole board tremble. The fury of his charge even makes the all-powerful queen think twice before approaching— especially when he's backed by his brother rook.

You see, rooks can move in both directions, along either ranks or files for as many open squares as they wish. Since they can both be on the same rank or file at the same time, they can support each other directly. In this situation, they are much more powerful than bishops or knights. In fact, when working together, they are even more powerful than the queen.

In the endgame, when the field is wide open, two rooks can easily mate the enemy king. When one of the rooks charges the king, the king drops his cup and the rook cries, *"Checkmate!"* And so ends the king and his cup.

Elephant Chess Anyone?

It is possible that chess originally came from China 1500 years ago. A game called Elephant Chess was played there at the time. The playing pieces were flat, and each had a special way of moving. They included kings, general, horses, wagons, and cannons.

Rook Strategy Tips

* Within your first ten moves, use one of your rooks for castling.
* For defense, keep a rook beside your king in the early part of the game.
* Rooks are strongest when connected, on the same rank or file, particularly at the end of the game.
* Use your rooks to defend your passed pawns.
* Keep your rooks free and ready to capture any opposing passed pawn that is about to be promoted to a queen.
* Use your rooks to support action on the center files d and e.

A Rook Gone Berserk?

The berserker was not known for his good manners. He was a special type of Norse warrior who raged in battle a thousand years ago in northern Europe. It is said that he tore into combat without armor or clothes, terrifying even the bravest enemy. Perhaps this rook, who is quietly gnawing on his shield represents a berserker. The piece is one of the famous Viking chess set, known as the Lewis Chessman.

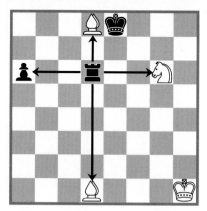

The rook can threaten four pieces at once.

QUIZ - What piece can the white rook capture safely?

A Moving Castle?

In India, well over a thousand years ago, the rook was a fierce chariot, pulled by many horses. More recently, it came to be thought of as a castle, and the special castling rules were also invented. We are now left with the funny picture of a moving castle. In making chess pieces, some artists have put the castle on wheels, and others on elephants, to show them moving. Still others turn the rook into a ship.

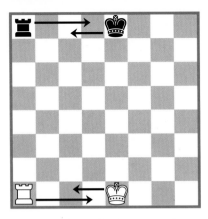

To castle queenside, first move the king two squares to the left, then move the queen's rook to the square directly right of the king.

Castling

Castling is a special defensive move that protects the king and brings the rook into play. It is the only time two pieces move on one turn.

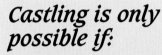

Castling is only possible if:

1. No piece or pieces are between the king and the rook.

2. The king is not in check.

3. The king and the castling rook have not moved since the start of the game.

4. The king does not move through or land on a square under attack.

Note: The king can castle, even though the castling rook is threatened.

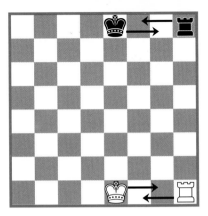

To castle kingside, first move the king two squares to the right, then move the king's rook to the square directly left of the king.

More about Castling

White cannot castle because the white king has moved.

White cannot castle because the king is in check from the black bishop.

Black can castle queenside, but not kingside, because the king would have to pass over a square threatened by white's bishop.

White cannot castle at this point because the square on which the king would land is under threat from the black bishop.

The white king can castle kingside, but not queenside because the rook has moved.

29

THE QUEEN

Queens like frightening kings, especially opponent kings. Kings take everything far too seriously. They forget that chess is, after all, just a game. As a result it is easy to scare them. Queens know this.

The queen is all powerful. With agility and speed she glides along the ranks, files, and diagonals of the board, moving in any of eight directions, and across as many open squares as she wishes. She fascinates all with her strength. As the game begins, she looms silently on her own square, a square of her own royal color, guarding her king and looking just the way a sovereign is supposed to look: aloof, majestic, proud, nose pointed high, seemingly quite disinterested in all this chess stuff. Of course, she is only pretending, and everyone knows it. No one dares ignore her, ever.

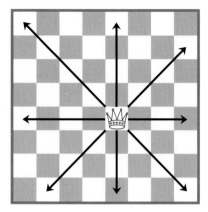

* The queen is the most powerful piece on the board. She combines the powers of the bishop and the rook.
* A queen can move in any direction, over as many empty squares as she wishes.

The queen knows better than to move too early in the game, while knights, bishops, and pawns crowd the board, fiercely jostling for position. Her every step would be dogged, her ability to sail gracefully over the squares would be limited, and she would soon need to retreat to safety. She could even be tripped by an impudent pawn, intent on the great honor of capturing her. It would be quite humiliating, really.

Indeed, sometimes the powerful queen herself falls. Great moans and wails resound throughout her kingdom, while the king wrings his hands in gloom and self-pity. The game goes on though. You see, it's only if the king is mated that the game ends; it's for this reason that the king insists on wearing the taller crown.

The queen has not said much about that — yet.

Once the board is clear enough for her to move, the queen sweeps down. All eyes nervously follow her moves. She pounces with dazzling speed when and where she chooses. In a flash, she sweeps into the enemy camp, wreaking havoc with a vengeance. Bishops tremble, knights stumble in fright, pawns gape terrified — perhaps those very pawns who dared each other to make faces at her, when they thought she wasn't looking.

Her *double attacks* are particularly feared. Because she can control squares in eight directions she can threaten many pieces at once. But always it is the enemy king she seeks, while wielding a mighty battle ax and gleefully crying, "Off with his head, off with his head!" It's enough to give any king real nightmares...

A Game of Queens

Chess is often called the game of kings, although it was a favorite game of many queens as well. Especially in the Middle Ages, chess was enjoyed by men and women alike, in all classes of society. The game was also very popular in the eighth and ninth century, among Arabian women and men.

Queen Strategy Tips

* Avoid using your queen too early in the game. Your opponent will simply chase her around the board.
* Always think and look carefully before you move your queen.
* Keep your queen from being blocked in by your own pieces or opposing pieces.
* Use your queen to defend your passed pawns, because each pawn can become a queen.

Amazing Sisters

Many children have become incredible chess players. Even when she was thirteen, it was being said of Judith Polgar that she would eventually win a match against the world's greatest chess champion. At fifteen, she was then the world's youngest grandmaster. Incredibly, she has two sisters, Susan and Sophia, who are also sensational chess players.

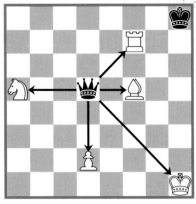

The queen can control up to 27 squares at once.

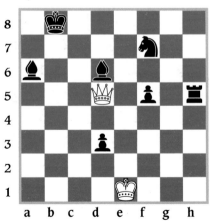

QUIZ — What piece can the white queen take and still not be taken herself in the next move?

Checkmate!

A queen, supported by any piece or even a pawn, can easily forge a king against any edge of the board.

THE KING

"Checkmate!!!" How every king quails at the finality of that horrible, game-ending word! It's so disagreeable. And all his subjects dread it, too. After all, if the king is captured, the kingdom is lost, and the game over.

Naturally, someone who is *this* important has to act with a certain amount of dignity. So, although the king can move in any direction he chooses, he does so only one square at a time, taking slow, careful strides and giving an impression of confidence and power. But the need to act with majesty does leave the king somewhat vulnerable. He can't simply run out of the way of an attack. He has to take only one step and then stand and wait for the next attack.

Every time an opposing piece threatens the king, the piece gets very excited and immediately cries, "Check!" That's the other word the king hates to hear, and so do the rest of his subjects.

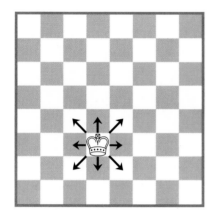

* The king is the most important piece you have: *always* protect the king.
* The king can move one square in any direction.
* The king may not move into check or be exposed to check by moving one of your pieces.
* If a move exposes your own king to check, the move cannot be made.

When "check" is declared, all other action on the board stops, and everyone looks toward the king. Can the king get out of check by himself? If he can't, the other pieces are ready to help: that is, if they can. The suspense can be awful, and very embarrassing for the king.

There are only three ways a king can get out of check: he or one of his subjects can capture the threatening piece; he can move one of his own subjects into the line of fire; or he can move to an empty square that is not under attack.

One of these things *must* happen. The most important rule in the game of chess is this: the king can never remain in check or be placed in check because of a move by himself or by one of his subjects. This rule is very important, because if the king cannot get out of check, a "checkmate" must be declared — and that means the game is over, and the king and kingdom are lost.

It is easy to see why the king doesn't do much throughout the game. Mostly, he just stays put on his royal throne, thinking about defenses that can keep him out of check. In fact, at the beginning of a game, he usually does not move at all. While his subjects struggle for the center of the board, he keeps a vigilant eye on the enemy's advance and heeds in particular the moves of any forward pawns.

When he thinks he knows which side the enemy will approach from, the king often makes his first move of the game. Usually, but not always, he will castle to the side opposite to his enemy's advances. Since castling can happen only if both he and his rook have not yet moved, the king does it as soon as he can, lest something should force either him or his rook to move, and thus destroy the opportunity. (See pages 28-29 for more information on castling.)

Castling often leaves the king sitting behind a wall of three watchful pawns, with the big, solid rook to one side and nothing but nice, safe, empty space to the other. Once the king has nestled himself into such a cozy position, he tries to avoid leaving it until the very end of the game. Not only is he safe here, the rook is wonderful company and makes excellent tea. From this position the king can rest up for the endgame while keeping a sharp lookout for the approach of any opposing pieces.

The security of this comfortable asylum rarely survives an entire game. As the battle rages on, sometimes the king wishes he wasn't the center of all the attention. He anxiously fidgets with his crown while the enemy captures more and more of his subjects. His queen may even have fallen, perhaps while protecting him against two rooks crashing into his defenses. And now his only remaining rook, the one at his side, has smashed down his Wedgwood cup, heaved his castle aloft, and gone tearing down a file, bellowing fiercely into the fray.

Finally comes an onslaught of attacks, a string of checks — enough to give anyone the heebie-jeebies. But if the king feels a little queasy while ducking each charge, he does not hide in corners! When most of the pieces who can defend him have vanished, including his castle pawns, the king finds the edge of the board a dangerous resting place. There he can easily be snared by as few as two opposing pieces, particularly if one of them happens to be a queen. He is safer if he advances toward the center. If there is still one remaining unfriendly bishop leering about, he carefully avoids the same color squares.

The king reviews the ways the battle might end. Of course, his being checkmated is one possibility —"Lose the battle and my poor head!" he thinks, "No, that would never do." And so, even in the darkest moments, he concentrates either on a victory, or on finding a clever way to force a truce, a "stalemate" or a "draw," in which no one loses. Chess has taught him courage.

It is now that the king swells with his imperial magnificence, a truly powerful force. Once away from the edge of the board, he can control eight squares at once. He looks for pawns, particularly passed pawns, whom he can support in an advance to the final rank. A pawn promotion often assures a speedy victory. Or else he plans how to support a checkmate of his opponent, which he can do if he backs his queen, or just one rook. Tonight, it's his turn to give someone else nightmares.

A Blocking Bishop

The king cannot castle because he would have to pass over a square controlled by the black bishop.

You Can Play It Blindfolded!

If you have a good memory, it is possible to win a game of chess without ever looking at the board. It is an amazing talent, and one in which U.S. Grandmaster George Koltanowski excelled. In Edinburgh in 1937 he played blindfolded against 37 opponents at once!

King Strategy Tips

* Try to castle early in the game on the side opposite your opponent's main attack.
* Watch for advancing opposing pawns in front of your king. They may attack your king.
* If you have castled, protect the three pawns in front of your king. They keep him safe.
* Use your king to defend your passed pawns.
* Near the end of the game with only pawns left, your king can march one or more pawns all the way to the other side for queen promotion.

QUIZ — What piece can the white king capture without putting himself in check?

The king controls up to eight squares.

The Game

Beginning the Game

You have now met all the pieces and read all the rules. The board is set up. Two lines of pawns stare at each other, and behind them, the royal pieces wait tense with anticipation. Now what happens?

The first part of a chess game is referred to as the opening or development. There are millions of possible openings to a game. Yet, of those possibilities, some are repeated so frequently they have names!

There are only a few simple strategies important to starting a game. Above all, pieces should develop their position to control the center four squares of the board. There are two good reasons for this. First, pieces are more powerful in the center. For instance, a bishop wielding his crook in the center of the board controls up to fourteen squares, while he controls only up to eight from the edge — where, incidentally, he can also more easily be trapped. Second, once in control of the center, pieces can readily shift their attacks to the queenside or the kingside, should the opponent king castle.

At the very start of play, only the pawns and the knights can move. The center pawns are often the first to spring into action, with bold double-square advances. Their moves free diagonals for the bishops, who quickly follow into play. The knights in particular enjoy this moment, eager to exploit their mischievous leaping skills, jumping over the helmets and miters that begin to crowd the center of the board.

While all the initial jostling for position takes place, the queen is patient. If she advanced too early, she could easily be surrounded on a crowded board. Her gliding moves would be restricted. She might even find herself awkwardly retreating from the poking lances of some presumptuous and pesky opponent pawns. Occasionally, however, she might take a small step in front of the king, to permit him to castle queenside.

Once the way is clear, it is time for the king to castle protecting himself behind a protective wall of pawns. This move also frees the rooks, but like the queen, rooks do not like being involved in the fray too early. They are usually quite happy minding the game from the turret tops, watching the action unfold, until some barb provokes them...

The center four squares are considered the most powerful ones on the chessboard. A game often begins with both sides struggling to control them.

Teamwork

As the pieces advance, they make sure they protect each other. By working together, they try to control as much of the board as possible, both by occupying important squares and by directing their firepower through as many squares as they can.

Pawn Chain

Pawn chains are formed by two or more connected pawns on the same diagonal. Pawn chains are difficult for an enemy to breech without losing a piece. A castled king can safely relax behind a "V" shaped pawn chain.

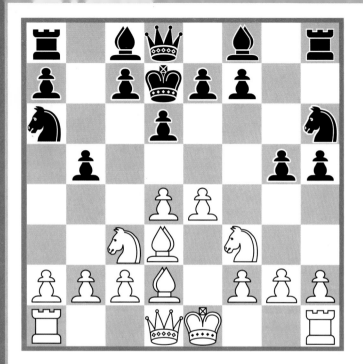

Strong and Weak Openings

White has opened well. Pawns, knights, and bishops have advanced to control the center of the board. Notice how well they protect each other. Finally, the king is ready for castling behind a row of protective pawns.

Black has opened badly. The pawns and knights seem to have moved without a plan. They do not protect each other and make no attempt to control the center of the board. The bishops remain powerless on their back rank, and no thought has been given to castling. In fact, the king cannot castle now, because he has already moved.

Is there a chess player in the house?

In medieval times, minstrels traveled from castle to castle. Some were professional chess players who carried their own boards. A lady or lord who enjoyed chess could match wits with a touring minstrel. Some even hired chessplayers to live in their own house!

Attacks and Exchanges

At any stage in the game, pieces may threaten each other with capture by attacking one another's positions. Sometimes, however, an attacking pawn or even a queen is so enthralled by the exciting possibility of capturing an opponent that they step directly on a dangerous square (one guarded by a lurking twinkling-eyed bishop perhaps), and thus perish for nothing.

When attacking, pieces must first and foremost always be prudent, and never advance onto a square where they can easily be taken without at least some sort of positional gain or favorable exchange.

To calculate the relative strength of pieces in an exchange, chess players refer to a point value system:

pawn = 1 point
knight = 3 points
bishop = 3 points
rook = 5 points
queen = 9 points

So if a knight captures a bishop and is then taken in the next turn, there is a fair exchange. But if the knight captures a rook before being taken in the next turn, then the knight's side has won the exchange. The chart should only be used as a rough guide though. Generally, developed pieces should not be swapped for undeveloped ones of the same point value, because a developed piece is always more powerful.

When you begin playing, here's a little number to keep in mind: the number of possible ways of playing the first ten moves is —
169,518,829,100,544,000,000,000,000,000.

At the beginning of the game, both sides will often develop their positions by threatening each other, but without actually capturing any pieces. Can you spot the possible exchanges?

Now let's turn the tables. What should an unprotected piece do when attacked? If nothing is done, the piece may be pinched from the board without compensation. In this situation *all* of the king's subjects consider five options, to see which are possible and which one is best:

1. The threatened piece may move out of the line of attack.

2. The threatened piece, or a fellow piece, may capture the attacker.

3. A fellow piece may block the attack.

4. A fellow piece may move to protect the threatened piece, so that, if it is captured, the attacker may be captured in exchange.

5. A fellow piece may attack an altogether different enemy piece in response. Now, if the threatened piece is captured, an enemy piece may still be captured in exchange.

QUIZ — It is white's turn to move. Black is attacking an undefended white pawn. How might white respond? (There are several possibilities.)

Sometimes a counterattack is the best defense. A pinned and unprotected knight is under double attack. Black cleverly responds by moving the bishop between white's king and rook. The king must move out of check, and a valuable rook is captured.

The Middlegame

In some of the most exciting games, not a single piece is captured throughout the opening. Instead, black and white pieces threaten and counter-threaten, defend and counter-defend, all while pouring out into the center of the battlefield. A great sense of agitation builds. Then as a zealous pawn pricks an opponent in the next file with his lance, a great brouhaha erupts, and the battle begins.

Time Out!

Professional chess players sometimes play with these two-sided clocks, to speed up the game. Otherwise, you are allowed to think for as long as you want for each move. If you are beginning to play, though, both you and your opponent should try to make quick decisions. At this stage, it keeps the game exciting, and you can learn a lot from the mistakes.

Simply rushing about attacking enemy pieces is not enough to win. Even placing the enemy king in check will not necessarily give much of an advantage. To develop a strong attack and to gain the upper hand, pieces need to work together and to exploit devious and sneaky tactics. Many tactics have names — the fork, the pin, and the discovered attack. All are particularly fierce when a king is one of the pieces threatened by them.

A Mathematician's Reward

According to legend, the emperor of China wanted to reward the inventor of chess. The inventor was allowed to name his own gift. He asked for one grain of rice for the first square of his chessboard, two for the second, four for the third, and so forth, doubling each time for each of the sixty-four squares. The request seemed small enough, and the emperor agreed. His mathematicians then calculated that this gift was more than every single grain of rice in all of China!

The Fork

The fork is a double attack by a single piece. It is most effective if the threatened pieces do not move or capture in the same direction as the attacker. A pawn, a bishop, or even a king, for example, can fork two knights or two rooks. A knight can fork any combination of two or more pieces, unless he meets another knight, of course. A knight is therefore the only piece that can use this tactic against a queen.

The black knight lands in front of the white bishop, and so threatens the white king and the white rook at once. This is a classic example of a powerful fork. Since the king must move, the rook is captured in the next turn.

QUIZ — In a single move, the white queen can threaten black's two bishops, and rook in a three-way fork. Can you find the move?

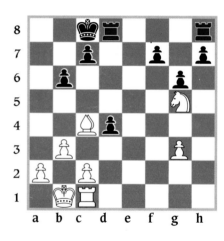

QUIZ — It is white's move. Can you spot a possible fork?

46

The Pin

The pin is a more subtle tactic, employed by the queen, rook, and bishop. It involves threatening two pieces on a single line of attack. The vulnerable piece in front cannot move without exposing a more valuable piece behind. If this more valuable piece is a king, then the first piece cannot move without exposing the king to check, which is illegal.

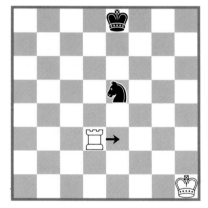

The white rook moves onto the knight's file and traps him in a pin. The knight now cannot jump aside to escape capture, because he would expose his king to check.

QUIZ— The black rook is trapped in a pin. It cannot move without exposing the king to check from the white bishop. It is white's move. Is it possible to capture the black pawn that is about to be promoted?

Queens are particularly fearsome in their ability to pin and capture unwary opponents.

The Skewer

Like the pin, the skewer is a tactical move employed by the queen, rook, and bishop. It involves threatening two pieces on a single line of attack. The piece in front is the more valuable one, usually the king, whose only defense is to move out of the way. The piece behind is thus exposed to the attack, and may be captured.

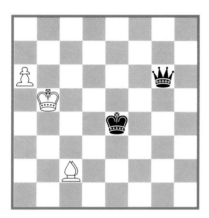

Black seems to have the advantage in this game until the white bishop moves to check the black king. Behind the king, and also on the bishop's diagonal, sits the black's unlucky queen. She can be captured in the following move, [...] the king must scurry aside to [...] check.

QUIZ — It is white's turn to play. Is it possible to capture black's queen in two moves? How can the black king best respond?

Plan Ahead

Chess games are inevitably full of surprises that disrupt even the most clever strategies. It is, however, best to have some sort of plan before you move each piece.

And don't forget to consider your opponent's plan. Watch the enemy carefully, and study every move. Can you guess what is being planned on the next move? Just as you can surprise your opponent, so can your opponent surprise you!

The Discovered Attack

The discovered attack is a kind of ambush. It is a surprise attack, which occurs when a non-threatening piece moves to reveal a threatening one. Like the pin, it is a tactic in which the long-range pieces specialize: the bishop, the rook, and the queen. If the piece moved also threatens a capture, then a *double attack* results.

If the discovered attack threatens the king, then it is *discovered check*. If both the moved piece and the revealed piece threaten the king, then it is a *double check*. In a double check, the king will always have to move.

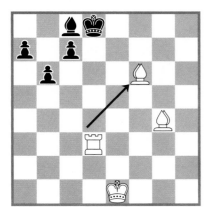

The white bishop moves to give a double check. Such an attack always forces the king to move, and here he must move away from the safety of his remaining defenses.

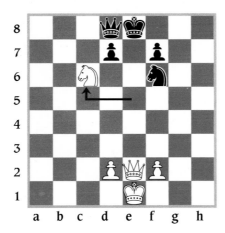

QUIZ — The white knight moves to reveal an attack by his queen on the black king. Can black save the queen from being taken in the next move?

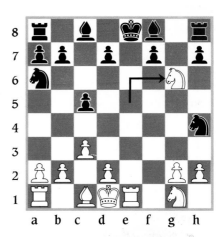

QUIZ — The white knight moves to threaten the black bishop and the rook in... Why... knight no... response?

The Endgame

As more and more pieces are captured and removed from the board, the pace of the game quickens and new strategies are needed. Whole ranks, files, and diagonals are opened, permitting the swift movement of the pieces, especially the bishops, rooks, and queens.

In the endgame, the remaining pawns gain importance, and the other pieces guard them well. At the end of a game a passed pawn can often strut gloriously to the final rank and be promoted to any piece (except, of course, a king).

At this stage of the game, the king may seem awfully exposed to the checks from the enemy. Yet it is precisely now that he may become particularly powerful and dangerous, supporting other pieces in attacks, and even helping the occasional checkmate. And more than once have passed pawns marched to promotion in the shadow of their king!

It happens too that the ravages of battle so reduce the pieces that, in the end, neither side has enough strength to checkmate the other. If two solitary kings remain on the board, for example, there could never be a checkmate, no matter how bravely one chases and the other retreats.

The following combinations of pieces are also unable to checkmate alone.

* **A king and a bishop**
* **A king and a knight**

But remember that a single pawn can make the difference: a pawn can be promoted, and even by itself can be critical in a checkmate.

Should a weakened king face forces any more formidable than these combinations, he may be doomed. The attacking army tries to reduce the number of squares he can move to, and nudges him to the edge of the board, where his movements are most limited.

Practice, Practice, Practice

Good endgame skills win many chess matches. To practice your skills, set up a few pieces on the board, giving one player the advantage. Start by practicing checkmating a lone king with a king and (1) a queen and a rook; (2) two rooks; (3) a queen only; (4) two bishops; and (5) a bishop and a knight. All these combinations should win.

To Promote a Pawn

In the endgame, the king will often expose himself to attack to protect a pawn on its way across the board. If this pawn can reach the final rank, then it can be promoted to a queen.

How Games End

Checkmates

When a king hears "Checkmate," he is not a little bewildered. A dumbfounded pause follows, then his royal eyes begin to dart, hither and thither. Surely there's been *some* mistake. But no. Only the silent and ever widening grins of his foes greet his eyes. Beyond them his remaining pieces, scattered uselessly beyond his reach, look on helplessly. There is no way around it. He can't move out of check, and no one can block the check or capture the piece giving check. The king is not "captured" like other pieces: the game simply ends, and the rest is left to his royal imagination.

Here is an example of an attack ending with a checkmate. The white bishop captures a pawn and threatens the black king. The king cannot block the attack, nor can he capture the bishop. The king's moves are limited by his own pawn and the edge of the board, and the two open squares he can move to are both attacked by the rook. White wins the game.

A king can often be checkmated on a crowded board. Here he finds himself gazing at the backs of his own pawns, which are blocking his way to safety. A white rook has advanced to deliver a swift "back-rank" mate.

Tipped over

A game can be lost without checkmate being declared. In a moment of grim hopelessness, when a checkmate is almost certainly looming, a king may be knocked over to admit defeat. This act is considered quite dignified, even though it is an act of resignation.

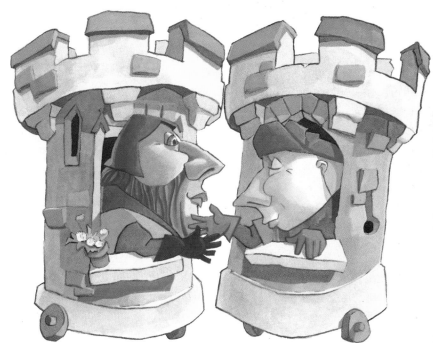

Companions at Arms

Rooks are strongest in the endgame, when they work together on either the same rank or file. A pair of rooks can very easily checkmate an unprotected king.

More about Checkmate

Learning to recognize checkmate patterns is one of the great keys to better chess playing. Here are two examples and puzzles showing different types of mates.

A queen, protected by a single piece, even a humble pawn, can easily checkmate a king on the edge of the board. Here the black queen moves to give checkmate, while being supported by her own king.

The knight may deliver a decisive checkmate when the king finds all of his movement choked by his own pieces. Here the king is about to be caught in a smothered mate.

QUIZ — The two rooks, working together on an open board, can also easily checkmate a lone king. To mate, what is black's next move?

QUIZ — It is simpler to checkmate a king if his movement is restricted by his own pieces, or by the edge of the board. In one move the white queen alone can give checkmate. Can you spot it?

The King's Back Door

A castled king knows that an opponent rook or queen can easily checkmate him on the back rank, if he is snuggled behind a line of three unadvanced pawns with no castle at his side. It's time to make a back door! He does this by asking one of his pawns to advance one square, thus giving him a safe escape off the back rank.

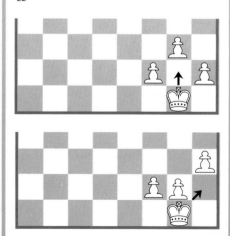

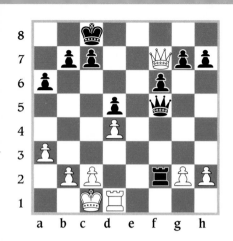

QUIZ — It's white's turn to move. Can you see the single move which will checkmate the black king in each of these six examples?

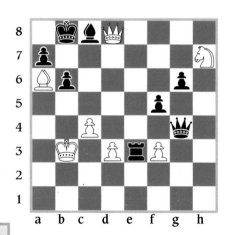

How Games End — CONT.
Draws

Not all games end with one king standing and the other tipped over in defeat. In fact, many games end in a draw, in which no one wins.

A draw can be a disappointing result if you have been long planning the sure downfall of your opponent with shrewd and devious tactics. However, should you happen to be losing — should your tired king be quaking in his ermine before the unstoppable, unleashed fury of mighty enemy rooks charging, or before the madness of an opponent queen capturing your pieces in a rage unstoppable — suddenly a draw might seem, to that very frightened king, to be the most exciting strategy ever. Chess teaches us the courage to look for possibilities until the very end.

We have already seen that sometimes both sides have lost so many pieces that, in the end, neither can checkmate the other. This is one kind of draw. There are other kinds. The agreed draw, stalemate, and perpetual check are all draws.

Computers That Play Chess

Can a computer beat the world's best chess player? For the last few decades, specialists have concentrated on building such a computer. It has been a very tough job, since chess is a such a complex game. In May 1997, the computer Deep Blue finally defeated Gary Kasparov, possibly the world's best ever chess player.

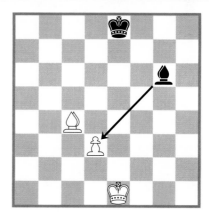

Black's move. Black decides to capture the pawn. He loses his bishop on the following turn, but the move ensures that white cannot win. White can no longer promote a pawn, and the remaining bishop and king are too weak to checkmate the lone black king.

Stalemate

A game might also end in a stalemate, in which case neither side wins. Suppose your king is not in check, but any move you make will put him into check. Because you cannot make a legal move, a stalemate is declared. If you are the stronger player in the game, and you are eagerly expecting a great victory, be wary of letting this happen. It's very upsetting to have a sure win snatched from your grasp! Sometimes a player even plans a stalemate if an ignominious and seemingly assured defeat is looming.

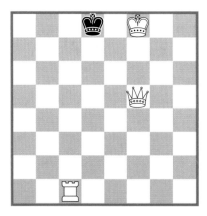

This overwhelmed black king is suddenly feeling quite relieved, even though he is surrounded. It is his turn to move, but he cannot do so legally — that is, he cannot move without putting himself into check. The game ends in a stalemate, which is a draw.

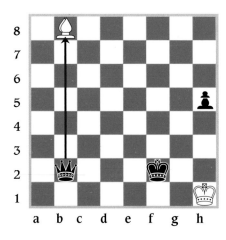

QUIZ — Black clearly has an advantage and should win the game. But the black queen moves too hastily and takes the white bishop. Why is this a very bad move?

Perpetual Check

A player who is losing might also look for a chance to place an opponent into perpetual check. In this case, a number of moves, usually two both checking the opponent king, can be repeated forever.

Other Draws

A game may be declared a draw by either player under two other circumstances. If the identical positioning of all the pieces on the board occurs on three occasions, at any time in the game, with the same player about to move each time, *a draw due to repeated position* may be declared. You would need to keep a good record of the game to call this kind of draw, as you would for *a draw by the fifty-moves rule*. This draw may be claimed if there have been fifty moves without any captures or pawn moves. It usually occurs at the end of a game. Both of these draws are fairly technical, and you need not worry much about them yet.

Finally, as in many games, you may have a draw by agreement. Perhaps, after a long time of play, you find yourself tired and unable to win any obvious advantage. Simply offer to draw. If your opponent agrees, the game ends.

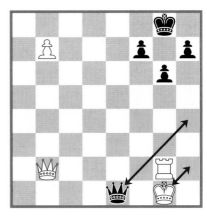

White is about to win the game through a pawn promotion. But the black queen forces a draw by placing the king into perpetual check. Even though he was about to win, the white king suddenly finds himself powerless. A draw is declared.

Chess Notation

A thousand years ago, Arab scholars began recording complete chess games for careful study later. We can still see every move they played! The system for recording a game is known as notation, and in its most popular form it is known as algebraic notation.

The Squares

In algebraic notation, each of the sixty-four squares on the board is given an address, consisting of a small letter followed by a number. The board is seen from the white side. Each file, from left to right, is identified by a letter (a-h), and each rank, from bottom to top, is identified by a number (1-8).

The Pieces

A piece is represented by a capital letter, the first letter of its name. The knight, as always, likes to be the exception. It is represented with its second letter N to avoid confusion with the king.

> king = K
> queen = Q
> bishop = B
> knight = N
> rook = R

Pawns do not always need a letter for identification if a position clearly tells of their moving.

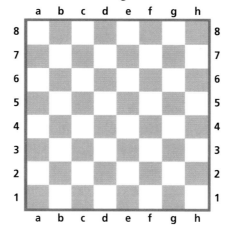

The Moves

In notation, each move begins with a letter that represents the piece, followed by the address to which that piece moves. Thus "Ra5" means the rook advances to file a, rank 5. If two rooks could have made this move, then an additional letter or number would be added to identify the rook. "R8a5" would mean that the rook on the eighth rank moves to a5.

Moves are numbered and recorded in pairs. White's move is listed first, followed by three dots, followed by black's move. For example a game might begin

> 1. e4 . . . Nf6
> 2. d4 . . . d5
> 3. Bd3

Some symbols are also used to show the development of the game. "X" indicates a capture. If the knight were to take the pawn from the above example on black's third move, the notation would read "3 ...Nxe4." An en passant capture is given its special notation "e.p." and it is written after the coordinates.

Here are some other symbols used:

o-o	kingside castling
o-o-o	queenside castling
=	pawn promotion
e.p.	en passant
x	capture
+	check
#	checkmate

The Fastest Game

The fastest checkmate can occur after only two paired moves. It is known as a "fool's mate." Can you work it out, using this notation?

    1. g4 ... e5
    2. f3 ... Qh4#

The Scholar's mate:

    1. e4 ... e5
    2. Bc4 ... Bc5
    3. Qh5 ... Nf6
    4. Qxf7#

The World's First Chess Computer?

In Vienna at the end of the eighteenth century, no one could beat this mechanical Turkish chess player. The box beneath him, which was full of wheels, cranks, and rods, was opened for the public to view. It appeared to be the first automatic chess machine, and it became very famous. In fact a person could hide in this box, behind false mirrors, and operate the Turk puppet with pulleys and levers — a trick not discovered for many years!

Chess Terms

Algebraic notation: A modern reference system for recording entire chess games.

Bad bishop: A bishop whose usefulness is reduced by its own pawns

Back rank mate: Checkmate by a queen or rook along the king's castling rank when the king is blocked by its own pawns.

Backward pawn: A pawn that has pawns of its own color on adjacent files only in front of it, having no other pawn for protection.

Capture: To remove an opponent's piece from the board by moving onto the square it occupies.

Castling: A special defensive move in which the king and one rook are allowed to move on the same turn.

Check: An attack on the opponent's king by either a piece or pawn.

Checkmate: A direct attack on the king, from which the king cannot escape in the following move. It marks the end of the game.

Closed file: A file blocked by two head-on black and white pawns.

Combination: A planned series of moves intended to force an opponent into an undesirable position.

Connected pawns: One pawn diagonally supporting another pawn.

Discovered attack: A move in which a non-threatening piece reveals an attacking piece behind it.

Discovered check: A move in which one piece reveals a second piece behind it that is attacking the king.

Double check: Occurs when a piece moves to put the opponent's king in check, revealing a second check by another piece.

Double pawns: Two pawns of the same color positioned on the same file.

Endgame: The closing stage of the game.

En passant: A special type of pawn capture that can occur after a pawn has initially moved two squares.

Exchange: Trading a piece for an opposing piece.

FIDE: Fédération International des Echecs. The World Chess Federation which organizes the International rating system, awards, and titles. Their highest title is International Grandmaster.

File: Any vertical column on a chess board.

Fixed pawn: A pawn whose advance is blocked by an enemy piece.

Fork: A simultaneous attack on two pieces by one enemy piece.

Good bishop: A bishop that is mobile and not blocked by its own pawns.

Illegal move: A move that does not conform to the rules of chess — usually a move into check or errors in castling.

Kingside: All squares on the e-h files.

Legal move: A move permitted by the rules of chess.

Mating net: Pieces working together to trap and checkmate the enemy king.

Middle game: The stage of the game after the opening and before the endgame.

Major piece: A queen or rook.

Minor piece: A bishop or a knight.

Mobility: The ability to move one's pieces to important parts of the board quickly and easily.

Move: Two turns — one by white and one by black.

Open file: A file on which there are no pawns. A file is still open even if it is occupied by pieces other than pawns.

Opening: The first stage of a game, from move one until piece development is complete.

Passed pawn: A pawn that will not encounter any opposing pawns on its own file or adjacent files.

Pawn chain: Two or more pawns of the same color along a diagonal.

Perpetual check: Occurs when a player is put in check repeatedly but cannot be checkmated. In this event the game is defined as a draw.

Pin: An attack on a piece that is shielding another piece of greater value, or a king.

Promote a pawn: Make a pawn into a more powerful piece (usually a queen, or sometimes a knight) when it reaches the other end of the board.

Promotion: When a pawn reaches the eighth rank, it must immediately become any piece except a king.

Queening square: The square a pawn must reach in order for it to promoted.

Queenside: All squares on the a-d files.

Rank: Any horizontal row on a chess board.

Resign: To surrender when faced with eventual, certain defeat.

Sacrifice: A tactic in which one piece is allowed to be captured so as to gain an advantage.

Smothered mate: A checkmate delivered by a knight when the king is blocked in by other pieces and/or pawns.

Underpromote: Promote a pawn to a piece other than a queen.

Quiz Answers

page 14: The white pawn captures the black pawn on e6.

page 19: The black pawn on c5 is captured by white's knight.

page 22: The black pawn on h7 is captured by white's bishop.

page 27: The black pawn on g4 is captured by white's rook.

page 32: The black knight on f7 is captured by white's queen.

page 38: The black bishop on e2 is captured by white's king.

page 44: (1) Threatened pawn could advance to f5 and avoid capture; (2) The threatened pawn could take the black pawn, and then be captured in exchange; (3) The king's pawn could advance one square, and so defend the threatened pawn.

page 46, middle: The white queen moves to e4.

page 46, far right: The white knight captures the pawn on f7 forking both black's rooks.

page 47: The black rook is also pinning the white rook. So the bishop can capture the black rook, and place the king in check. The white rook would then be free to capture the advanced pawn on h2.

page 48: The white rook advances to a6 to check white's king. The king must move, and the queen is captured. The black king's best defensive response is to move to g7 by the queen, so that he may capture the rook on the next move

page 49, middle: No, the queen will be captured.

page 49, far right: The king must first respond to a discovered check from the white rook on e1.

page 55, left: The black rook moves to a1 and mates white's king.

page 55, right: The white queen moves to h6 giving mate to black's king.

page 56, top left: The white queen gives mate on e8.

page 56, top middle: White's queen captures pawn on g7 and gives mate.

page 56, top right: White's pawn advances one square to g7 and gives mate to black's king.

page 56, bottom left: White's queen captures black's bishop on c8 and mates black's king.

page 56, bottom middle: The white pawn advances one square to f8 and promotes to a queen or rook giving mate.

page 56, bottom right: The white knight moves to f6 giving mate.

page 58: By taking the white bishop, the queen has forced a stalemate. The king cannot move. The game is a draw, though black could have easily won. For example:

    1. ... Qb7+
    2. Kh2... Qg2#